67890

1 2 3
MOOSE

A PACIFIC NORTHWEST COUNTING BOOK

PHOTOGRAPHS BY
ART WOLFE

TEXT BY
ANDREA HELMAN

SASQUATCH BOOKS
SEATTLE

1 wolf

This gray wolf pup stays warm and dry inside his thick fur coat. His sharp ears and loud howl will keep him in touch with other wolves.

2 moose

Though they're still too young for antlers, these long-legged Alaskan moose calves are already great runners and swimmers. Their big, floppy lips are just right for nibbling on trees or slurping up plants from rivers and lakes.

3
cougars

Cougars, or mountain lions, are strong, shy, and curious cats. They usually hunt at night, tiptoeing silently through the forest.

4 muskox

The "musky sheep-ox" really does smell musky! Protected from the cold arctic air by thick woolly hair, muskox huddle together during blizzards, sheltering their calves in the center of a tight circle.

5 *trumpeter swans*

Downy baby swans, called cygnets, hatch with their eyes open and take their first swim soon afterward. When they are three months old, they begin their flying lessons.

6 horses

These horses run free in Eastern Washington.
Long ago, when wild horses roamed the Northwest,
the Native Americans of the region became expert riders.

prong-
horns

Pronghorns bound through the prairie grass, traveling quickly and quietly. Thick pads on their hooves act like rubber soles, protecting them from rocks and thorns.

8
sea otters

Sea otters spend most of their time in the ocean. They float on their backs to eat, cracking open shells or munching spiny sea urchins. When it's time for a nap, the otters wrap themselves in strands of kelp so they won't float away.

9
paintbrush

Can you find the nine yellow flowers?
Paintbrush comes in reds and oranges and
yellows and pinks. This colorful plant grows in
meadows and marshes, on mountaintops,
and by the seashores of the Northwest.

10 scallop shells

Each of these shells once had a small animal called a scallop living inside.
Some scallops glue themselves to rocks and stay put. Others scoot along the
sea bottom by opening and closing their shells.

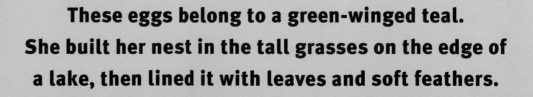

11 duck eggs

**These eggs belong to a green-winged teal.
She built her nest in the tall grasses on the edge of
a lake, then lined it with leaves and soft feathers.**

12
berries

Native Americans mashed these juicy but sour Oregon grape berries into flat cakes. Early pioneers made jelly and wine from them.

13
Bohemian waxwings

The Bohemian waxwing has brilliant spots on its wing feathers that look like drops of red wax. During courtship, the male and female pass a berry back and forth, from beak to beak, but never eat it!

14 owls

Pygmy owls and snowy owls, barn owls and spotted owls, hoot owls and screech owls—all of them can see in the dark, hear the softest sounds, and fly silently through the night.

15

male mallards

Count the glossy green heads of the male mallards. The brown female ducks are not nearly so flashy! Mallards feed day and night, using their sensitive taste buds to get the full flavor of bugs, acorns, and berries.

16

sea lions

Sea lions have poor eyesight, but still catch lots of fish. They glide through the water, flapping their front flippers like a bird flaps its wings, then haul themselves out on warm rocks to bask in the sun.

17
red-legged kittiwakes

These tiny gulls nest in large colonies on cliff ledges near the ocean. During courtship, males and females cling to the narrow ledges, rub each other's bills, and call "kitt-i-waak!"

18
river rocks

Can water change the shape of rocks? Yes! Rushing rivers, grinding glaciers, and hammering waterfalls jumble and tumble the stones about, wearing them down until they are smooth and round.

19

bears

Brown bears, black bears, grizzly bears, polar bears, and Kermode bears. The Northwest is home to many types of bears. They forage for fish, hunt for meat, and still have room for plants, fruit, insects, and honey.

20 bald eagles

Eagles don't usually stand around in groups—unless there is a salmon feast close by. Each winter thousands of bald eagles flock to Alaskan rivers and wait for the next run of spawning salmon.

12345

too many to count!

Can you count the pine cones in this picture? They come from the ponderosa pine tree, a large tree named for its ponderous, or heavy, wood.

For my six good friends and co-workers, Chris, Craig, Deirdre,
Gavriel, Mel, and Ray. You'll always be #1 in my book. —A.W.

Four my favorite folks, Sam and Adelle
To the twosome I could always count on
All my love, from A to Z. —A.H.

Published by Sasquatch Books.
Distributed in Canada by Raincoast Books Ltd.
Printed in Hong Kong.
Designed by Kate L. Thompson.

Library of Congress Cataloging in Publication Data
Wolfe, Art.
          1,2,3 Moose : subtitle/ photographs by Art Wolfe ; text by
          Andrea Helman.
                    p. cm.
          ISBN 1-57061-078-9
          1. Northwest, Pacific—Juvenile literature.
2. Alaska—Juvenile literature. 3. English language—Counting—
Juvenile literature. [1. Northwest, Pacific. 2. Alaska. 3. Counting.]
I. Helman, Andrea. II. Title.
F851.W76 1995
428.1—dc20   94-43908
[E]

SASQUATCH
BOOKS

1008 Western Avenue
Seattle, Washington 98104
(206) 467-4300

Sasquatch Books publishes high-quality adult
nonfiction and children's books related to the
Northwest. For information about our books,
contact us at the above address.

too
many
to
count!

Can you count the
pine cones in this
picture? They come
from the ponderosa
pine tree, a large
tree named for
its ponderous, or
heavy, wood.

For my six good friends and co-workers, Chris, Craig, Deirdre,
Gavriel, Mel, and Ray. You'll always be #1 in my book. —A.W.

Four my favorite folks, Sam and Adelle
To the twosome I could always count on
All my love, from A to Z. —A.H.

Published by Sasquatch Books.
Distributed in Canada by Raincoast Books Ltd.
Printed in Hong Kong.
Designed by Kate L. Thompson.

Library of Congress Cataloging in Publication Data
Wolfe, Art.
     1,2,3 Moose : subtitle/ photographs by Art Wolfe ; text by
     Andrea Helman.
          p. cm.
     ISBN 1-57061-078-9
     1. Northwest, Pacific—Juvenile literature.
2. Alaska—Juvenile literature. 3. English language—Counting—
Juvenile literature. [1. Northwest, Pacific. 2. Alaska. 3. Counting.]
I. Helman, Andrea. II. Title.
F851.W76 1995
428.1—dc20   94-43908
[E]

 SASQUATCH
BOOKS

1008 Western Avenue
Seattle, Washington 98104
(206) 467-4300

Sasquatch Books publishes high-quality adult
nonfiction and children's books related to the
Northwest. For information about our books,
contact us at the above address.